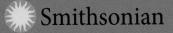

APOLLO 11:
Mission to the Moon

Courtney Acampora

Contents

Earth's Moon 3

What Is a Moon? 4

The Space Race 6

NASA.. 8

Learning About the Moon 10

The Apollo Program................................. 12

Apollo 11... 16

The Journey Home..................................... 24

After Apollo 11 26

Apollo 11's Legacy 28

Quiz 30

Glossary.. 32

Earth's Moon

At night, Earth's **moon** is the largest and brightest object in the sky.

For thousands of years, people stared at the night sky and dreamed of what it was like on the Moon's surface.

Fifty years ago, that dream came true when the first humans stepped foot on the Moon.

What Is a Moon?

Moons are objects that **orbit** planets. Some planets have many moons, but Earth has only one.

About every twenty-seven days, the Moon completes an orbit around Earth. The Moon causes the Earth's ocean tides.

Most scientists believe the Moon was formed a long time ago when a large object smashed into Earth. The collision broke off chunks of Earth that flew into space. The pieces joined together to form Earth's moon.

The Space Race

The Space Race was a competition between the United States and the Soviet Union.

Both countries wanted to prove they could go the farthest and the fastest in space exploration.

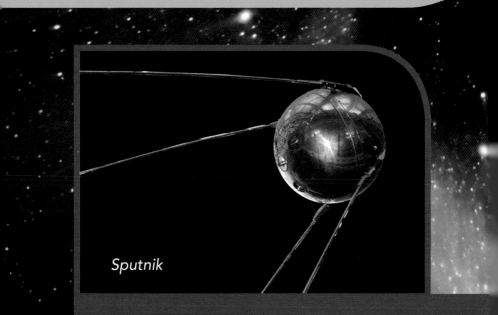

Sputnik

In 1957, the Soviet Union launched the first artificial **satellite**, Sputnik.

Then, in 1961, Russian **cosmonaut** Yuri Gagarin became the first human in space. He orbited Earth for one hundred and eight minutes.

Because of Gagarin's success, the United States became more determined to beat the Soviet Union in the Space Race.

NASA

After Sputnik's launch, President Dwight Eisenhower signed a law that created NASA in 1958. NASA stands for National Aeronautics and Space Administration.

NASA is a government agency that focuses on aviation technology and space exploration. NASA demonstrated the United States' dedication to winning the Space Race.

President Dwight Eisenhower (center)

*President
John F. Kennedy*

On May 25, 1961, President John F. Kennedy requested that the United States' Congress support a program to land humans on the Moon and return them home safely by the end of the decade.

Learning About the Moon

Before humans could go to the Moon, NASA needed to learn more about it. They needed to know if it was safe to land machines or humans on the Moon.

They sent **spacecraft** to the Moon that took photos, mapped and tested the surface, and collected soil samples.

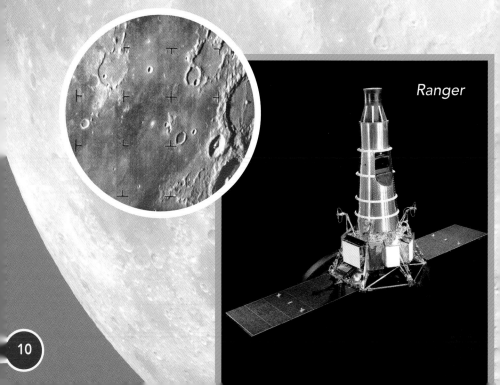

Ranger

NASA-S-65-893

Gemini capsule

Project Mercury was NASA's first human spaceflight program. Just one person flew in the tiny Mercury capsules.

Project Gemini followed with a two-person capsule. **Astronauts** practiced docking in orbit and learning how to live in space long enough to reach the Moon and return safely.

Apollo 1 crew

Several missions happened before Apollo 11. The first crewed Apollo mission was scheduled for early 1967, but sadly a fire killed the astronauts inside the **command module** during a preflight test.

In 1968, NASA launched Apollo 7. The crewed command and service module orbited Earth one hundred and sixty-three times and spent more than ten days in space.

The Apollo Program

Apollo 8 was the first mission to carry humans to orbit the Moon and back.

The crew did not land on the Moon, but they were the first people to see Earth from space with their own eyes!

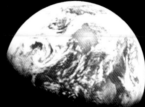

Apollo 9 tested the **lunar module** with a crew in place. The crew orbited Earth for ten days.

Apollo 10 was a complete rehearsal for Apollo 11, but did not land on the Moon.

NASA was ready for Apollo 11—the mission that would land the first humans on the Moon!

Apollo 11

On July 16, 1969, at the Kennedy Space Center in Florida, a Saturn V rocket carrying the Apollo 11 crew took off.

The crew included commander Neil Armstrong, command module pilot Michael Collins, and lunar module pilot Edwin "Buzz" Aldrin Jr.

Michael Collins

Neil Armstrong

Buzz Aldrin

Only three parts of what launched on the Saturn V went to the Moon.

The command module, *Columbia*, was the crew's quarters.

The service module held support systems and propelled the craft.

The lunar module, *Eagle*, took the crew to the Moon's surface.

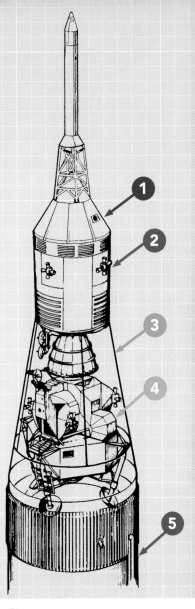

1 Command module
2 Service module
3 Spacecraft/lunar adapter
4 Lunar module
5 Launch vehicle

Apollo 11

Twelve minutes after takeoff, the crew entered Earth's orbit. They orbited Earth one and a half times.

Then, they were boosted out of Earth's orbit toward the Moon. It took three days to enter the Moon's orbit.

In the afternoon of July 20, 1969, the lunar module detached from the command-service module and began its descent to the Moon.

Apollo 11

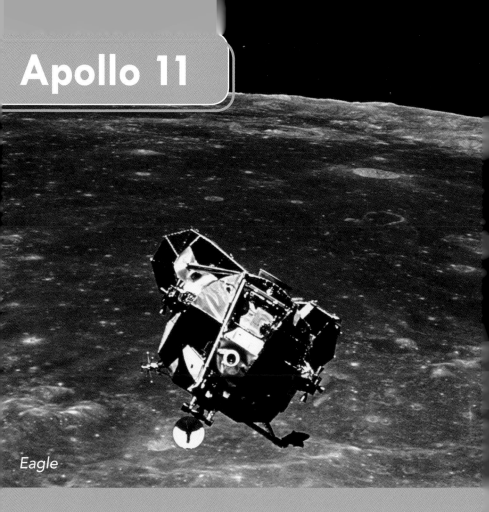
Eagle

Neil Armstrong and Buzz Aldrin landed on the Moon in *Eagle*. They landed in a flat area of the Moon called the Sea of Tranquility that was formed from ancient lava flows.

Michael Collins stayed inside *Columbia* and continued orbiting the Moon.

Before exiting *Eagle*, Armstrong and Aldrin prepared the lunar module for its stay on the Moon.

The schedule called for the astronauts to rest for five hours after landing, but the astronauts skipped it. They were ready to step on the Moon!

Buzz Aldrin on the Moon

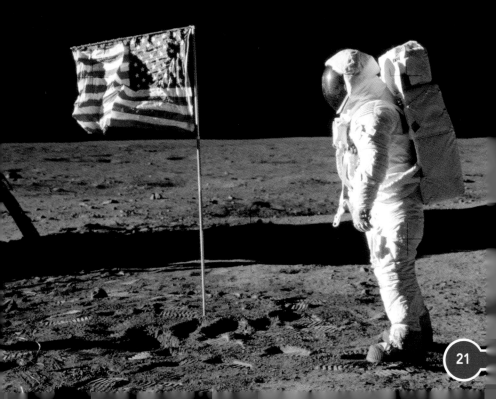

Apollo 11

On July 20, 1969, astronaut Neil Armstrong took the first steps on the Moon.

He said, "That's one small step for [a] man, one giant leap for mankind."

Later, Buzz Aldrin joined Neil Armstrong on the Moon's surface. They collected samples, did experiments, and took photographs.

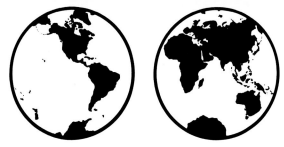

HERE MEN FROM THE PLANET EARTH
FIRST SET FOOT UPON THE MOON
JULY 1969, A. D.
WE CAME IN PEACE FOR ALL MANKIND

NEIL A. ARMSTRONG
ASTRONAUT

MICHAEL COLLINS
ASTRONAUT

EDWIN E. ALDRIN, JR.
ASTRONAUT

RICHARD NIXON
PRESIDENT, UNITED STATES OF AMERICA

The astronauts spent a little more than twenty-one hours on the Moon. Two and a half hours were spent outside *Eagle*.

The astronauts left behind an American flag, a patch honoring the Apollo 1 crew, and a plaque.

They left behind their bootprints, too!

The Journey Home

Neil Armstrong and Buzz Aldrin took off from the Moon and connected with Michael Collins in *Columbia*.

The crew left the Moon's orbit on July 21st, and three days later, landed in the Pacific Ocean near Hawaii.

The crew was taken immediately to a mobile **quarantine** facility. Scientists wanted to make sure the astronauts did not bring Moon bacteria back with them.

After eighty-eight hours inside the quarantine facility, the astronauts were transferred to the Lunar Receiving Laboratory in Houston, Texas. They stayed there for the remainder of the planned twenty-one day quarantine period.

After Apollo 11

An astronaut in a lunar rover

After the success of Apollo 11, six more Apollo missions were sent to the Moon.

Apollos 12, 14, 15, 16, and 17 conducted more scientific experiments, collected samples, and explored farther from the lunar module using a Moon car called a lunar rover. Apollo 13 was unable to land because of a malfunction (but the astronauts made it home safely).

In 1972, Apollo 17 was the last mission to the Moon. Since then, no humans have stepped on the Moon.

President John F. Kennedy's goal was met. NASA refocused its work on new technologies and exploring other parts of the solar system.

Apollo 11's Legacy

Apollo 11 was an important event because it showed humanity's ability to go beyond Earth with courage and bravery.

Apollo 11 paved the way for future exploration of even farther reaches of the solar system.

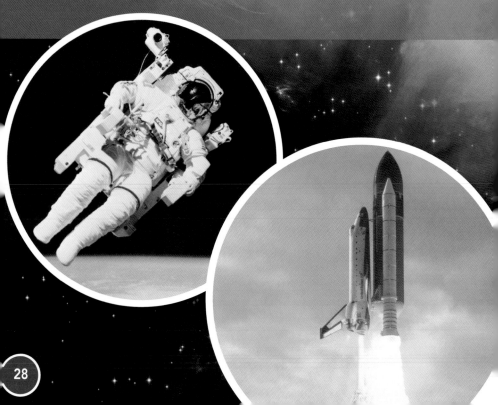

Millions of people watched Neil Armstrong take the first steps on the Moon. This goal took less than ten years to achieve, and suggests that almost anything is possible.

Apollo 11 has fueled the desire to explore planets, stars, and galaxies far, far away.

APOLLO 11: Misson to the Moon

QUIZ

1. What was the Space Race?
   a) A competition between the Soviet Union and the United States to prove who was the best in space exploration.
   b) The launching of two rockets to see which was faster.
   c) A race to see how fast Yuri Gagarin orbited Earth.

2. What does NASA stand for?
   a) National Aerospace Science Academy
   b) North American Space Association
   c) National Aeronautics and Space Administration

3. Who declared that the United States should land a human on the Moon by the end of the 1960s?
   a) President Dwight Eisenhower
   b) President John F. Kennedy
   c) Yuri Gagarin

4. Where did Apollo 11 launch from?
   a) Florida
   b) Texas
   c) California

5. Which two astronauts were the first to land and walk on the Moon?
   a) Buzz Aldrin and Michael Collins
   b) Neil Armstrong and Michael Collins
   c) Neil Armstrong and Buzz Aldrin

6. What did the Apollo 11 crew NOT leave on the Moon?
   a) American flag
   b) Plaque
   c) Lunar rover

Answers: 1) a 2) c 3) b 4) a 5) c 6) c

GLOSSARY

astronauts: people who are trained to live and work in space

command module: control center and living quarters during lunar missions

cosmonaut: astronaut from the Soviet space program

lunar module: vehicle for landing on the Moon

moon: natural satellite that orbits a planet

orbit: path of a planet, moon, or spacecraft around another body

quarantine: a period of isolation

satellite: an object that orbits a planet, including human-made spacecraft

spacecraft: vehicle or device made for traveling outside Earth's atmosphere